Amphibious Vehicles

by Michael Green

Reading Consultant:
Sergeant James Petersen (retired)
United States Air Force

CAPSTONE PRESS

MANKATO, MINNESOTA

C A P S T O N E   P R E S S
818 North Willow Street • Mankato, Minnesota 56001

Printed in the United States of America.

Library of Congress Cataloging-in-Publication Data
Green, Michael, 1952-
    Amphibious vehicles/by Michael Green.
    p. cm. — (Land and sea)
    Includes bibliographical references and index.
    Summary: Discusses the history and military use of several amphibious
    vehicles, highlighting specific models and their roles in various battles.
    ISBN 1-56065-460-0
    1. Motor vehicles, Amphibious--Juvenile literature. 2. World War, 1939-
1945--Amphibious operations. 3. Vietnamese Conflict, 1961-1975--
Amphibious operations. [1. Motor vehicles, Amphibious. 2. Vehicles,
Military.] I. Title. II. Series: Land and sea (Mankato, Minn.)

V880.G74 1997
623.7'475—dc21

                                                                96-24272
                                                                CIP

Photo credits
FMC: 6-14, 18, 20, 25, 26
U.S. Army: 22
U.S. Marine Corps: 17, 28, 33-38
U.S. Navy: 4, 30, 41, 47

Table of Contents

Features

Pronunciation guides follow difficult words, both in the text and in the Words to Know section in the back of the book.

Chapter 1

Amphibious Vehicles

An amphibious (am-FIB-ee-us) vehicle can be operated on land or in water. Amphibious vehicles get their name from animals called amphibians. Frogs, toads, and salamanders are amphibians. Amphibians spend part of their life in water and part of their life on land.

Amphibious Soldiers

The United States Marine Corps (KOHR) has been the biggest user of amphibious vehicles. Marine means water. U.S. Marines are trained to fight at sea and on land.

Amphibious vehicles are used on land and in the water.

The marines depend on the U.S. Navy to get from ship to shore. The navy supplies small boats for this job. They have been using amphibious vehicles since 1941, when the United States entered World War II (1939-1945).

Amphibious vehicles have been used in many wars around the world. They have been improved over the years. The Marine Corps sees a strong future for new amphibious vehicles.

The Need for Amphibious Vehicles

In the 1920s, the U.S. Marine Corps began to see Japan as a threat. This was shortly after World War I (1914-1918) had ended. The Japanese navy was growing. The Japanese army had started to build military bases on islands in the Pacific Ocean.

In the 1930s, the Marine Corps began planning for a future war against Japan. The

Amphibious vehicles have been used since World War II.

Early amphibious vehicles, like this amphibious tractor, could cross only small rivers and streams.

marines knew they would have to capture Japanese-held islands. The marines wanted an amphibious vehicle that could be used in the water and on land.

8

Sizing Up the Future Battlefield

Many islands in the Pacific Ocean were surrounded by coral reefs. Coral is the hard and often brightly colored deposits of some ocean animals. Coral reefs are walls of these deposits near the ocean surface.

Boats could not travel over the coral reefs. But amphibious vehicles could climb over them without damage. They could then drive onto the beach.

During the 1920s and 1930s, other countries tested amphibious tanks. Tanks are enclosed vehicles protected with heavy armor. Tanks are mounted with various weapons, one of which is usually a large cannon. For extra traction, tanks move on tracks. Tracks are metal belts that run around wheels on both sides of a vehicle.

The amphibious tanks of the 1920s and 1930s could cross only very small rivers. The marines wanted a vehicle that could survive in the ocean.

ROEBLING AMPHIBIAN TANK

UNITED STATES NAVY

FOOD MACHINERY CORP

Chapter 2

Invention and Inventor

In 1938, the marines found the amphibious vehicle they needed. It was a rescue vehicle designed to cross swamps in the Florida Everglades. The inventor of this rescue vehicle was Donald Roebling (ROBE-ling).

Roebling came from a family of famous engineers. His grandfather was the builder of the famous Brooklyn Bridge in New York. His great-grandfather designed the bridge.

Roebling's First Amphibians

Roebling built his first amphibious vehicle in 1934. It was 24 feet (seven meters) long and

Donald Roebling designed this amphibious vehicle. It was called the Alligator.

11

10 feet (three meters) high. It was powered by
a Chrysler engine.

Roebling's vehicle was made out of
aluminum. Aluminum is a lightweight metal
alloy. An alloy is a mixture of two or more
metals. Aluminum is used to build cars,
airplanes, tanks, and many other things that can
benefit from less weight.

On land, Roebling's vehicle could travel 25
miles (40 kilometers) per hour on its tracks.
The tracks were shaped like scoops. In the

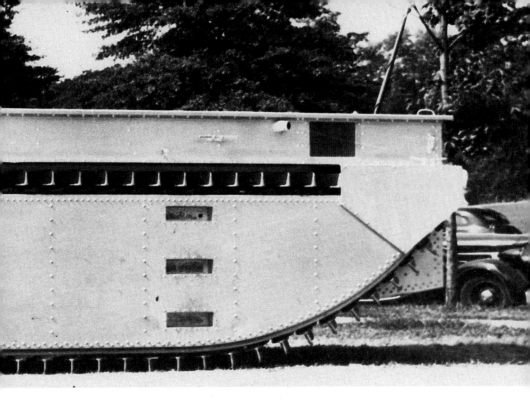

Roebling's vehicle had tracks shaped like scoops.

water, the tracks acted like hundreds of small paddles. Roebling's first amphibious vehicle had a top speed in the water of two and one-half miles (four kilometers) per hour.

Roebling wanted something that could go faster in the water. He built and tested two more vehicles in 1937. One of these vehicles appeared in *Life* magazine on October 4, 1937.

The Marine Corps Takes Notice

The marines noticed the story in *Life* magazine. Some of them decided to visit Roebling in Florida. They wanted to see his amphibious vehicle in action. The marines were convinced that the vehicle was right for them.

Roebling soon designed a new test vehicle for the marines. It was based on the experience gained from his earlier work. The vehicle was now named the Alligator.

When finished, the Alligator was 20 feet (six meters) long and eight feet (two meters)

This Marine Corps test Alligator had a 37mm cannon.

wide. It could climb over coral reefs and small hills. Its water speed was eight to 10 miles (12 to 16 kilometers) per hour.

Design Problems

The Marine Corps tested Roebling's Alligator. They found two problems. The first problem was that the aluminum construction would not stop enemy fire. The second problem was that the Alligator's tracks wore out too fast.

The navy asked Roebling to redesign his vehicle with steel instead of aluminum. Steel is stonger than aluminum. Roebling asked a company named FMC to help him redesign the Alligator. FMC was a builder of farm machines.

FMC built two test vehicles out of steel. The navy was happy with their test results. They ordered hundreds of the redesigned Alligators. The Marine Corps could use them in the Pacific Ocean.

The first of FMC's Alligators came off the assembly line in July 1941. A total of 1,225 Alligators were built during World War II. No other country has ever built a better amphibious vehicle than the FMC Alligator. Vehicles based on its concept continue to serve the Marine Corps today.

Today's amphibious vehicles are based on the Alligator.

Chapter 3

The Alligator Goes to War

Roebling's Alligator was officially known as the Landing Vehicle Tracked (LVT 1). A Marine Corps training unit was set up in May 1941. The unit taught marines how to operate the Alligator. Mechanics learned how to keep them running.

The Alligator was first used during wartime in August 1942. It brought supplies from ship to shore. But the steel was not thick enough to stop bullets. In attacks against Japanese-held islands, the Alligator suffered heavy losses of both cargo and crew.

The first wartime use of the amphibious Alligators came during World War II.

Redesigned Alligators

The marines decided they needed a more protected version of the Alligator. So two new armored Alligators were built to replace it. Armor is anything used to protect vehicles, people, and cargo during combat. Armor is usually made out of steel.

The first new armored vehicle was a cargo carrier nicknamed the Water Buffalo. A cargo carrier is a vehicle that carries supplies and ammunition. The Water Buffalo was also known as the LVT 2.

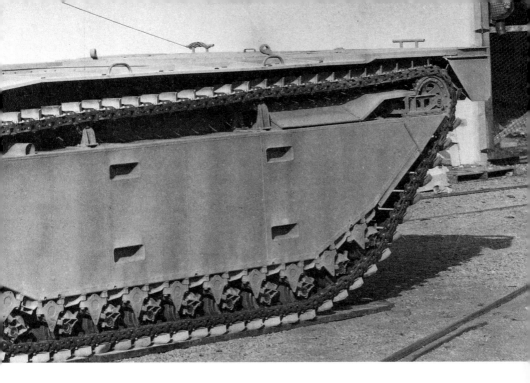

This amphibious vehicle was called the Water Buffalo.

The other new vehicle was an Alligator with steel armor and more weapons. It was fitted with a turret from a U.S. Army tank. A turret is a revolving armored wall that protects guns and gunners inside it. This vehicle was known as the LVT(A) 1.

The turret on the LVT(A) 1 held a 37 millimeter (mm) cannon. The millimeters measure the diameter of the cannon's barrel.

The 37mm cannon fired a two-pound (one-kilogram) shell. The turret also had a single machine gun. At the rear of the armored Alligator, two more machine guns were mounted.

More Design Problems

In 1943 and 1944, the Marine Corps captured many Japanese islands. They relied heavily on amphibious vehicles during the captures. The marines found more problems with the vehicles.

One big problem was the location of the cargo space. The early amphibious vehicles had the engines in the rear of the vehicles. There was no direct path to the cargo space, which was in the center of the vehicle. All cargo had to be lifted over the sides.

The lack of rear doors in these early amphibious vehicles caused other problems. In combat, marines had to jump or climb out of the vehicles. This was very dangerous if the

The Marine Corps used amphibious vehicles to capture many Japanese islands during World War II.

enemy was shooting at them. The marines suffered heavy troop losses until the problem was fixed.

Improving the Amphibians

The engineers went back to their drawing boards. They redesigned the amphibians with a rear ramp. The redesigned LVT 2 became the LVT 4.

The ramp made it easier to load or unload troops and cargo. Small trucks and cannons could be carried in the new amphibians. The engine was moved to the front of the vehicle to make room for the new ramp.

A Bigger Cannon

The 37mm cannon was also a problem. It could not shoot far enough. Marines had to get too close to the enemy to shoot at them. Losses were heavy when the amphibians got too close.

Engineers mounted a 75mm cannon on the Alligator. It fired a larger and more powerful shell. The 75mm cannon had a range of two

The LVT 4's ramp made loading and unloading easy.

miles (three kilometers). The Alligator with the bigger cannon was known as the LVT(A) 4.

The LVT(A) 4 could fire its cannon while in the water. Marines needed this ability when

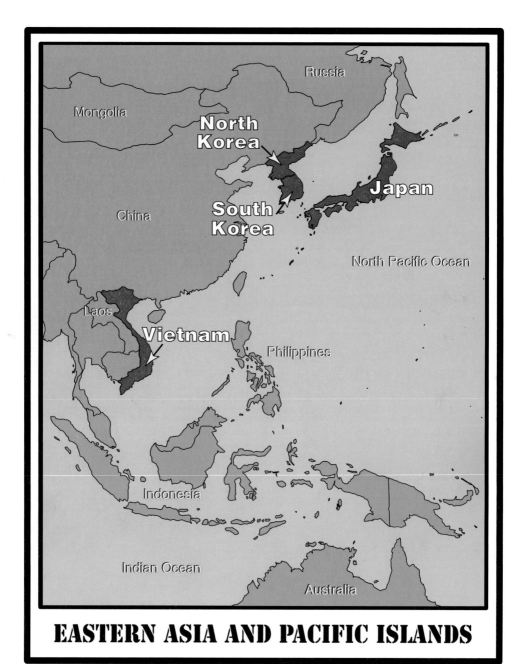

EASTERN ASIA AND PACIFIC ISLANDS

they were headed toward an enemy-held beach. Once on shore, the long-range cannon could protect other marines moving inland.

The turret on the LVT(A) 4 had an open top. This was not a problem in the water. But on land, enemy soldiers could throw hand grenades into the turret.

So an extra machine gun was fitted in the turret to protect it. It was one soldier's job to use the machine gun to kill any enemies close enough to throw grenades.

Iwo Jima

Iwo Jima is an island in the Pacific Ocean. It was controlled by the Japanese during World War II.

The U.S. Marines used amphibious vehicles when they captured Iwo Jima in 1945. The Marines lost many soldiers. Iwo Jima was one of the last islands captured by U.S. forces during World War II.

The battle at Iwo Jima is famous for a photo showing U.S. soldiers raising their country's flag after the victory. Many statues have been made to look like the photo.

Chapter 4

Postwar Amphibious Vehicles

After World War II, the marines began looking for a new amphibious vehicle. In 1945, such a vehicle was built by the Borg-Warner Company. It was called the Bushmaster. It was officially known as the LVT 3.

The vehicle's engines were mounted on both sides of the hull. The hull is the main body. On land, the vehicle could reach a top speed of 17 miles (27 kilometers) per hour. In the water, the

The LVT 3 was also called the Bushmaster.

The LVT 5 could carry up to 34 combat-ready troops.

Bushmaster had a top speed of six miles (10 kilometers) per hour.

The Bushmaster could carry as many as 30 combat marines and their equipment. Extra armor plates could be attached to the Bushmaster. A version of the Bushmaster was used during the Korean War (1950-1953).

Another New Vehicle

In 1950, the Borg-Warner Corporation began testing another vehicle. The new vehicle was supposed to perform many different jobs.

Borg-Warner began production of their new amphibious vehicle in 1952. It was known as the Landing Vehicle Tracked, Model 5, or LVT 5. The main job of the vehicle was to carry troops. It could carry up to 34 combat marines and their equipment.

The LVT 5

The LVT 5 was made of thin steel. It was shaped like a box. The engine was in the rear. There was a large ramp at the front.

The LVT 5's top speed on land was 25 miles (40 kilometers) per hour. In the water, it was propelled by its tracks. Its top speed in the water was six miles (10 kilometers) per hour.

The driver and commander of the LVT 5 sat at the front of the vehicle. The only protection the vehicle had was a single machine gun.

Different Versions

One version of the new LVT 5 was armed with a 105mm cannon. This vehicle was used to protect troop carriers.

The 105mm cannon on the LVT 5 could be fired at sea or on land. The vehicle could carry 90 rounds of ammunition. One round is one shot.

Another version of the LVT 5 was filled with radios and maps. It was used as a command-post vehicle. From such a vehicle, marine officers could control all their troops and vehicles.

The strangest-looking LVT 5 version was a combat-engineer vehicle. Combat engineers move and change the land to help soldiers during battles. A huge V-shaped bulldozer blade was mounted on the front of the combat-engineer vehicle. The blade was designed to move land mines and earth.

LVT 5 Problems

A problem with the LVT 5 was the location of its fuel tanks. They were at the bottom of the vehicle. If an LVT 5 drove over a land mine, the vehicle exploded and burned.

**The combat engineer version of the LVT 5 had a blade
designed to move earth and land mines.**

During the Vietnam War (1954-1975),
LVT 5s suffered high losses from mines. Many
marines refused to ride them. These and other
problems led to the call for another new
amphibious vehicle.

Chapter 5

Safer Amphibious Vehicles

Problems with the LVT 5 led to the new LVT 7. FMC designed and built the LVT 7 in the early 1970s.

As with the LVT 5, there were different versions of the same basic vehicle. Most of the LVT 7s were troop carriers. A repair version of the LVT 7 had a large crane attached to it. There was also a command-post version of the LVT 7.

The LVT 7 was first built in the early 1970s.

Turret

Winter Camouflage

C23

Tracks

The LVT 7
(Training in Norway)

Grenade Launcher

Hull

This LVT 7 has a machine gun mounted on top.

The LVT 7's three-man crew was made up of a commander, a driver, and a machine gunner. The LVT 7 could carry up to 25 combat troops and their equipment.

The LVT 7

The LVT 7 was built of armored aluminum. It was powered by a large diesel engine. Diesel is a fuel similar to gasoline. Diesel engines last longer than gasoline engines. They also travel more miles per gallon (kilometers per liter) of fuel. Diesel fuel is less likely to explode if struck by a mine or enemy fire.

On land, the LVT 7 had a top speed of 45 miles (72 kilometers) per hour. Over rough terrain, it had a top speed of 25 miles (40 kilometers) per hour.

The LVT 7 had a ramp in the rear. Marines and cargo can also enter or leave the vehicle through large top hatches.

In the Water

In the water, the LVT 7 was powered by two large waterjet pumps. These pumps were located at the rear of the vehicle. Earlier amphibians used only their tracks to move in the water.

The waterjet pumps mounted in the LVT 7 took in water from above the tracks. The water was pushed out under high pressure at the rear of the vehicle. This moved the vehicle through the water. On land, the LVT 7 waterjets were turned off.

The Assault Amphibian Vehicle

In the early 1980s, the marines had the LVT 7s rebuilt. They also decided to change the name. They called the new version of the LVT 7 the Assault Amphibian Vehicle (AAV).

The AAV had a more powerful engine. It also had an improved suspension system, which gave troops a smoother ride when the vehicle drove over the land.

To make the AAV safer, the marines added new armor. The new armor was made of plastic rather than heavy steel. The special plastic armor protects AAV passengers from many weapons.

Future Amphibious Vehicles

The Marine Corps continues to improve its AAVs. The marines hope to use them until the year 2004. By then, they plan to have a more advanced vehicle.

The marines want a vehicle that goes faster through the water. It must also have improved armor to protect troops from bullets and

This LVT 7 is mounted with a grenade launcher.

bombs. The new vehicle must have a light but powerful cannon. Instead of a diesel engine, it might have an electric motor. The new vehicle will carry the marines into the next century.

Words to Know

aluminum (uh-LOO-mi-nuhm)—a lightweight metal alloy

armor (AR-mur)—anything used to protect vehicles, people, and cargo during combat

cargo carrier (KAR-goh KA-ree-ur)—a vehicle that carries supplies and ammunition

combat-engineer vehicle (KOM-bat EN-juh-nihr VEE-uh-kuhl)—any vehicle that combat engineers use to move and change the landscape to help soldiers during battles

command-post vehicle (kuh-MAND POHST VEE-uh-kuhl)—any vehicle from which military officers control their troops and vehicles in combat

diesel engine (DEE-zuhl EN-juhn)—an engine that burns diesel fuel rather than gasoline

Roebling, Donald (ROBE-ling DON-uld)—the man who invented the first amphibious vehicle, which became known as the Alligator

tank (TANGK)—enclosed vehicle protected with heavy armor

tracks (TRAKS)—metal belts that run around wheels on both sides of a vehicle

troop carrier (TROOP KA-ree-ur)—wheeled or tracked vehicles that carry soldiers

turret (TUR-it)—a revolving armored wall that protects guns and gunners inside it

waterjet (WAW-tur JET)—a system by which water is sucked in at one end of a device and then pushed out the other end at a high speed

To Learn More

Chant, Christopher. *The Marshall Cavendish Illustrated Guide to Military Vehicles*. New York: Marshall Cavendish, 1989.

Foss, Christopher F. *Jane's Armored Personnel Carriers*. London: Jane's Publishing, 1985.

Mesko, Jim. *Amtracs*. Carrollton, Texas: Squadron/Signal Publications, 1994.

Zaloga, Steven. *Amtracs: U.S. Amphibious Assault Vehicles*. London: Osprey Publishing Limited, 1987.

Useful
Addresses

Amphibious Tractor Museum
Joint Public Affairs Office
Marine Corps Base
Camp Pendleton, CA 92055

History and Museum Division
Headquarters U.S. Marine Corps
Washington, DC 20380

U.S. Navy Public Affairs Office
1200 Navy Pentagon
Room 2E341
Washington, DC 20350-1200

Virginia Museum of Military Vehicles
Aden Field
Nokesville, VA 22123

Internet Sites

The Great War Society
http://www.mcs.net/~mikeil/tgws/

Normandy Photos Database
http://144.99.192.2401/Normandy/
NormandyPhotos.html

The United States Marine Corps
http://www.usmc.mil/

World War II Stories
http://www.islandnet.com/~awong/war/
index.html/

The LVT 5 was used by the U.S. Marines in the Vietnam War.

Index